IS-1101.B: Basic Agent Tutorial

By

Fema

12/18/2017

Lesson 1 Course Overview

This course provides an introduction to the essentials of flood insurance.

Objectives: At the end of this course, you will be able to:

- Apply knowledge of the National Flood Insurance Program in order to answer customer questions and resolve issues
- Build an NFIP policy while taking the necessary community, building, coverage and rating options into consideration
- Locate and use NFIP resources

Lesson 1 Objectives

This course is organized into five lessons. Lesson 1 will introduce you to the essentials of flood insurance. This lesson provides:

- A basic knowledge of the National Flood Insurance Program (NFIP)
- An awareness of the NFIP's mission
- An overview of flood risks found on a Flood Insurance Rate Map (FIRM)

Frequently Asked Questions

The **Basic Agent Tutorial** will prepare you, the flood insurance agent, to answer your clients' questions.

Here are some frequently asked questions about the NFIP:

1. How do I know if I am in a high-risk flood zone?
2. Can I purchase flood insurance even if I do not live in a high-risk area?
3. Do I have to wait for an official presidential disaster declaration before I can file a claim?
4. Will my flood policy cover my home and belongings?
5. Are the contents in my basement covered?
6. After the flood, my shop couldn't open for two weeks. Does my flood insurance policy cover our loss of business income?
7. I have a Standard Flood Insurance Policy. Am I guaranteed a Replacement Cost Value loss settlement?

How the NFIP Works

The NFIP's mission is to reduce the consequences of flooding by making flood insurance available to property owners and encouraging communities to establish floodplain management programs, by adopting minimum regulations for development in flood hazard areas.

Select this link to view the FEMA National Flood Insurance Program website.

How to Access the NFIP

The NFIP offers the following two options for obtaining coverage:

- Through Write Your Own insurance companies (also known as WYOs) which are private sector insurance carriers that function under an arrangement with the Federal Emergency Management Agency (FEMA) to sell flood insurance for the NFIP, or
- Through the NFIP Servicing Agent (also referred to as the NFIP Direct since it allows agents to write business directly through the NFIP)

Write Your Own

WYOs write policies under their own name and give every impression that they are the actual carrier. They issue the policies, collect the premiums, renew the policies, and endorse them. When there are losses, they handle their own claims. However, these carriers are at no underwriting risk whatsoever.

WYOs are one way that you as an agent can access the NFIP—by striking an agreement to write flood insurance through them. There are a variety of small and large WYO Companies from which to choose.

Select this link to view a complete list of WYO insurance companies.

Community Participation

Now that you know you can access the NFIP through WYOs and the NFIP Direct, the next question becomes: **Who can buy flood insurance?**

The key to who can buy flood insurance revolves around the concept of community participation and a partnership between the community and FEMA.

Community Participation (cont'd)

FEMA makes flood insurance available in communities that agree to participate in the National Flood Insurance Program.

In turn, participating communities agree to adopt and enforce floodplain management regulations and Flood Insurance Rate Maps (FIRMs). These regulations guide development in a community's flood prone areas. By using better building practices, the community reduces the impact of future flooding.

A **Flood Insurance Rate Map (FIRM)** is the official map of a community on which FEMA has delineated the Special Flood Hazard Areas (SFHAs), the Base Flood Elevations (BFEs), and the risk premium zones applicable to the community.

Community Participation (cont'd)

When a community participates in the NFIP, it participates in one of two phases: the Emergency Program or the Regular Program.

Emergency Program: Entry-level participation phase.

- Limited coverage
- Flat rates
- Basic Flood Hazard Boundary Map (FHBM)*

Regular Program: Most participating communities are in this phase.

- Full participation
- Detailed Flood Insurance Rate Map (FIRM)
- NFIP's full limits of insurance

---

*Initial flood hazard identification

Does My Community Participate?

FEMA maintains a listing of communities that participate in the NFIP called a Community Status Book.

Select this link to view the Community Status Book.

Select a state or U.S. territory in the Community Status Book and a list of participating and non-participating communities will be presented along with each community's participation details, which we will review next.

Community Status Book

Select this link to view the Community Status Book. Click on any state to preview the columns discussed below.

CID: A different community identification number is assigned for the incorporated city versus the unincorporated county. You must determine where the building is physically located to know which community to look up.

Community Name: Again, we're looking at the incorporated city or unincorporated county, parish, or borough.

County: This column should match the relative incorporated city, township, village, or other entity.

Init FHBM Identified: This date tells when the Flood Hazard Boundary Map was created. This map is only a factor in communities that do not have a Flood Insurance Rate Map.

Init FIRM Identified: This date represents the community's first Flood Insurance Rate Map, and it is important because it represents the dividing line between two building categories called Pre-FIRM and Post-FIRM, which we will discuss in more depth later in this course.

Curr Eff Map Date: This is the date of the map currently in effect.

Reg-Emer Date: The date the community first joined the NFIP. An "E" next to the date indicates that the community is in the Emergency Program and subject to limited coverage. If there is no "E" next to the date, then the community participates in the Regular Program.

Tribal: A "yes" in this column indicates that the participating community is a tribal nation.

Activity

Here are some tasks to help you become familiar with the Community Status Book.

1. Find the community status listing for your community
2. Determine whether your community participates in the Emergency or Regular Program
3. Locate the community identification number (CID) for your community
4. Identify the initial FIRM date for your community

<u>Select this link to view the Community Status Book where you can complete the above tasks.</u>

Flood Insurance vs. Disaster Assistance

What are the differences between flood insurance and disaster assistance?

Flood Insurance

- Flood insurance from the NFIP puts the policyholder in control
- Flood insurance claims are paid even if a disaster is not declared by the President

Disaster Assistance

- The most common form of federal disaster assistance is a loan that must be paid back with interest
- The duration of a Small Business Administration (SBA) disaster home loan can extend to 30 years

By allowing the policyholder to make decisions about coverage limits and deductible options, NFIP flood insurance puts the property owner in control.

Flood Zone Basics

Flood zones fall into two categories: **Special Flood Hazard Areas** (SFHAs) and **Non-Special Flood Hazard Areas** (Non-SFHAs). SFHAs are the most flood-prone zones. These are also the zones where federally regulated and insured lenders must require the purchase of flood insurance as a condition of a loan.

Flood Zone Basics (cont'd)

Characteristics of an SFHA:

- "100-year floodplain" with 1% annual chance of flood
- At least a 26% chance of flooding over a 30-year mortgage
- High-risk zones are designated as either A zones or V zones

Flood Zone Basics (cont'd)

V Zones

V zones* are typically found in coastal areas. The V stands for velocity, which means there is wave action with the water.

———————

*Includes Zone V, Zones V1-V30, Zone VE

Flood Zone Basics (cont'd)

Non-SFHAs

The Non-Special Flood Hazard Areas are represented on flood maps by Zones B, C, and X. These are more moderate- to low-risk areas.

There is no federal statute requiring the purchase of flood insurance in these zones. However, more than 20% of NFIP losses occur outside of mapped Special Flood Hazard Areas.

What is a FIRM?

The Flood Insurance Rate Map (FIRM) is the official FEMA map of flood zones and Base Flood Elevations.

Select this link to view the FEMA Flood Map Service Center.

Activity

FEMA Flood Map Service Center (MSC)

Have you visited the MSC? <u>Select this link to view the FEMA Flood Map Service Center.</u>

Next we'll learn how to use the MSC to find an online version of a Flood Insurance Rate Map. It may be helpful to start out by searching for a familiar location such as your home or office address. Follow the search prompts and click on the help buttons to view your Flood Insurance Rate Map.

<u>Select this link to view a job aid with step-by-step instructions on creating a FIRMette, a small portion of a Flood Insurance Rate Map.</u>

Coastal Barrier Resources System (CBRS)

Before we leave the topic of flood maps and flood zones, we will discuss the Coastal Barrier Resources Act. This law protects our natural resources.

In 1982 and again in 1990, Congress enacted legislation that prohibits federal expenditures or financial assistance, including flood insurance, in certain designated Coastal Barrier Resources Systems (CBRS's) and Otherwise Protected Areas (OPAs).

It is important to know whether a building in one of these areas was built <u>before</u> or <u>after</u> the area was identified. Buildings constructed or substantially improved after the identification date may be ineligible to purchase flood insurance (even in participating communities).

A list of communities where CBRS's and OPAs have been identified can be found in the NFIP Flood Insurance Manual.

Additional Resources

Here are some resources mentioned in this lesson. Select each resource to learn more:

National Flood Insurance Program

Write Your Own Flood Insurance Company List

NFIP Community Status Book

FEMA Flood Map Service Center

NFIP Flood Insurance Manual

Lesson 1 Summary

This lesson presented an overview to broaden your knowledge of flood insurance essentials including:

- The NFIP's mission to make flood insurance available to property owners through Write Your Own insurance carriers and the NFIP Direct in a mutual partnership with local communities.
- An overview of flood risks found on Flood Insurance Rate Maps.

The next lesson presents information on understanding the Standard Flood Insurance Policy.

Lesson 2 Objectives

In this lesson, you will review:

- The Standard Flood Insurance Policy forms and coverage
- The standard 30-day waiting period and exceptions
- The NFIP definition of flood

Your Clients' Questions

Next, we will review some questions your clients may have about the Standard Flood Insurance Policy (SFIP):

- How many policy forms are there?
- What defines a flood event?
- What does my policy cover?
- How are deductibles handled?

Types of Policy Forms

The Standard Flood Insurance Policy (SFIP) consists of three coverage forms:

1. The Dwelling Form
2. The General Property Form, and
3. The Residential Condominium Building Association Policy (RCBAP) Form

Knowing how the building is used helps you know which policy form applies to that building.

Dwelling Form

The **Dwelling Form** applies to a non-condominium residential building designed for principal use as a dwelling place for one to four families, or to a single-family dwelling unit in a condominium.

General Property Form

The **General Property Form** is used to insure a non-residential building* or a 5-or-more-unit residential building not eligible for the Residential Condominium Building Association Policy (RCBAP). This form is also used to insure non-residential contents in any building or a building owner's residential contents located in multiple units within a building with 5 or more units.

*For rating purposes, non-residential buildings are classified as either **Non-Residential Business** or **Other Non-Residential** buildings. See the General Rules Section of the NFIP Flood Insurance Manual for a complete definition of each category.

Residential Condominium Building Association Policy (RCBAP)

The **Residential Condominium Building Association Policy** is used to insure a building which is owned and administered as a condominium, contains one or more units, and in which at least 75% of the floor area is residential. The building must be located in a Regular Program community.

Preferred Risk Policy (PRP)

The Preferred Risk Policy, also known as the PRP, is a rating option with specific eligibility and documentation requirements:

- The building must be in a moderate- to low-risk zone B, C, or X or in flood zones AR or A99 to be eligible
- Since it is a preferred product, the building must meet certain loss eligibility requirements which apply to any 10-year period regardless of change of ownership
- The PRP requires upfront eligibility documentation which is submitted along with the application

The PRP can be written on an individual condominium but not condominium associations. It applies to all other buildings categorized as residential and non-residential.

It is important to recognize that the PRP does not use a different coverage form but rather relies on the Dwelling Form or General Property Form for outlining coverage. The PRP is not a separate set of products—it is a different rating option for writing flood insurance. It is a simplified approach which can result in a lower cost.

Waiting Period

Once you collect the premium and complete the flood insurance application, coverage does not necessarily take effect immediately. The Flood Insurance Manual provides guidance about when coverage actually begins.

There is a 30-day waiting period before many new or modified flood insurance policies go into effect (30 calendar days, not business days). However, there are three exceptions to this rule. Next, we will discuss each exception.

Waiting Period (cont'd)

Exception 1

No Waiting Period (Loan Transaction)

The most frequent exception to the 30-day waiting period occurs when flood insurance is purchased in connection with a loan. Flood insurance that is initially purchased in connection with the making, increasing, extending, or renewal of a loan shall be effective at the time of loan closing, provided that the policy is applied for at or before closing.

Waiting Period (cont'd)

Exception 2

1-Day Waiting Period (Map Revision)

A map change from a Non-SFHA to an SFHA is the basis of this second exception. If an insured purchases coverage within 13 months of a new map, the waiting period is reduced to one day.

Waiting Period (cont'd)

Exception 3

Post-Wildfire Conditions

Finally, a third exception was added as a part of the Biggert-Waters Flood Insurance Reform Act of 2012. The 30-day waiting period does not apply if a property has been affected by flooding from Federal land that was caused by post-wildfire conditions.

Policy Term

The policy term for a Standard Flood Insurance Policy is one year for policies written through the NFIP Servicing Agent or a WYO company.

Cancellations

Flood insurance coverage may be terminated by either canceling or nullifying the policy in accordance with a valid reason for the transaction, as described in Paragraph I.B., *Valid Reason Codes of Cancellation/Nullification of NFIP Policies*, in the Cancellation section of the NFIP Flood Insurance Manual. If coverage is terminated, the insured may be entitled to a full or partial refund under applicable rules and regulations.

For more details, select this link to review the NFIP Flood Insurance Manual and refer to the Cancellation section.

NFIP Definition of Flood

A common question asked by policyholders is:

What type of flooding has to happen before I can file an NFIP policy claim?

In order to answer that question, first we need to review the definition of flood.

NFIP Definition of Flood (cont'd)

The NFIP's definition of flood is:

"A general and temporary condition of partial or complete inundation of two or more acres of normally dry land area or of two or more properties (at least one of which is your property) from:

- Overflow of inland or tidal waters;
- Unusual and rapid accumulation or runoff of surface waters from any source;
- Mudflow; or
- Collapse or subsidence of land ... as a result of erosion or undermining caused by waves or currents of water ... that result in a flood as defined above."

NFIP Definition of Flood (cont'd)

Mudflow is included in the definition of flood. In the aftermath of such an event you would see a dried-out riverbed where the mud flowed through in its liquid state.

Mudflow is defined as a river of liquid or flowing mud on the surfaces of normally dry land areas as when earth is carried by a current of water.

NFIP Definition of Flood (cont'd)

Collapse or Subsidence

The Standard Flood Insurance Policy also covers the collapse or subsidence of land along the shore of a body of water as a result of erosion or undermining caused by waves or currents of water exceeding anticipated cyclical levels that result in a flood.

Remember, the collapse or subsidence of land (including erosion) must be a direct effect of a flooding condition as defined by the NFIP.

Types of Coverage

Let us explore some basics about the policy forms that the NFIP offers. We will talk a little bit about what a flood insurance policy covers as well as what it does not cover.

As part of this topic, we will discuss the three different coverage forms.

Types of Coverage

There are four types of coverage available under the Standard Flood Insurance Policy:

Coverage A: Building Property

Coverage B: Personal Property

Coverage C: Other Coverages

Coverage D: Increased Cost of Compliance

Next we will take a look at each of these coverage areas.

But First ... What is a Building?

The NFIP's definition of a building is rather broad. A building must meet the following criteria to be eligible for coverage:

- Have at least two rigid exterior walls and a fully secured roof
- Be affixed to a permanent site (resist flotation, collapse, or lateral movement)
- Be principally above ground level

Buildings in the Course of Construction

Buildings in the course of construction, alteration, or repair can also be considered buildings for coverage purposes. The NFIP does not have a separate builder's risk form, but each of the three coverage forms has coverage wording that allows for buildings in the course of construction.

Coverage can apply even before the building meets the requirement of having "two rigid exterior walls and a roof." Some other important things to know are:

- Coverage is offered while work is in progress, or up to 90 days after work is halted
- Building deductible is doubled (until the building is walled and roofed)
- No coverage is offered if the lowest floor is below the Base Flood Elevation (BFE)

Additions and Extensions

Now that we know the NFIP's definition of a building, we can take a look at additions and extensions to the building.

The coverage forms state that a "building" includes any addition or extension attached to or in contact with the building by means of:

- A rigid exterior wall
- A solid load-bearing interior wall
- A stairway
- An elevated walkway
- A roof

The Standard Flood Insurance Policy coverage forms state that: "At [the insured's] option, additions and extensions connected by any of these methods may be separately insured." This gives the insured the latitude to increase the amount of coverage by purchasing more than one policy.

Detached Garage

Now that we know what a building is and how we handle additions and extensions, what about structures appurtenant to buildings?

The NFIP allows you to write one building per policy. So, if you have five buildings, you have to write five policies. There's only one exception to this. The exception is found only in the Dwelling Form, and it only applies to detached garages.

Here's how it works. At the time of loss, the insured has the option to extend up to 10% of the Coverage A building limit to the detached garage. However, if the garage is used or held for use for **residential, business, or farming** purposes, it is <u>ineligible</u> for the extension and must be insured separately.

Coverage A: Building Property

The Standard Flood Insurance Policy provides a sampling of items covered under the Coverage A limit. While the list is not exhaustive, it does illustrate the types of property that would always be considered "building property" rather than personal property.

Here are some items that are covered only under Coverage A—Building Property:

- Awnings, canopies, and outdoor antennas
- Blinds and permanently installed wall mirrors
- Built-in dishwashers and microwaves
- Carpet permanently installed over unfinished flooring
- Central air conditioners, furnaces, radiators, hot water heaters, including solar water heaters
- Elevator equipment and fire sprinkler systems
- Permanently installed cupboards, bookcases, cabinets, paneling, and wallpaper
- Plumbing fixtures, garbage disposal units, and pumps
- Walk-in freezers, ranges, cooking stoves, ovens, and refrigerators

Coverage B: Personal Property

Let us transition over to Coverage B – Personal Property.

Personal Property is not automatically included with the purchase of building coverage. Make sure you offer this important coverage. Your client can buy building only, personal property only, or both.

Coverage B: Personal Property (cont'd)

Dwelling Form
The Dwelling Form provides coverage for personal property inside a building at the described location (if the property is owned by the insured or their household family members) and, at the insured's option, the property owned by their guests or servants.

Coverage B: Personal Property (cont'd)

General Property Form and RCBAP

It should be noted that on both the General Property Form and the Residential Condominium Building Association Policy (RCBAP), the personal property must be inside a **fully enclosed insured building** to be covered. The additional latitude provided to the insured on the Dwelling Form does not apply to the other two coverage forms.

Coverage B: Personal Property (cont'd)

Examples of Personal Property Items

We will review the types of items that are covered under Coverage B. This is not an exhaustive list but it does illustrate that items on the list will always be considered personal property items.

Included in the sample list provided in the Standard Flood Insurance Policy are:

- Air conditioning units (portable or window)
- Carpets, not permanently installed, over unfinished flooring
- Carpets over finished flooring
- Clothes washers and dryers
- Cook-out grills
- Freezers (not walk-in), food in any freezer
- Portable microwave ovens, dishwashers

Did you notice? A portable or window air conditioner is a personal property item while a central air conditioner is considered a building property (Coverage A) item.

Coverage B: Personal Property

General Property Form: Household Property vs. Non-Household Property

Next we will highlight an important aspect of the General Property Form related to Coverage B. A variety of buildings and occupancy types can be insured under the General Property Form, so the form offers the option to cover either "household" (residential) items **or** "other than household" (commercial) items (but not both).

If a policy covers "household" personal property, it will insure:

- Typical household personal property
- Property belonging to the insured or to a family member
- Property for which the insured may be legally liable

If a policy covers "other than household" personal property, it will insure:

- Furniture and fixtures
- Machinery and equipment
- Stock
- Other property the insured owns and uses in a business

Basement Coverage

Definition

Before we leave our discussion of Coverage A and B, let us throw one more thing into our building—a basement. We will start by taking a look at the NFIP definition of a basement.

A **basement** is defined as any area of the building, including any sunken room or sunken portion of a room, having its floor below ground level (subgrade) on all sides.

It does not matter what anybody living there calls the area or does with it—if the floor is subgrade on all sides, then it meets the definition of a basement.

Basement Coverage (cont'd)

Building Items Covered

Why is understanding the basement definition so important? It is because there are coverage limitations in basements.

The "building" items covered in a basement under Coverage A include:

- Central air conditioners
- Cisterns and the water in them
- Unfinished drywall (walls, ceilings) **in a basement**
- Electrical outlets, switches, junction and circuit breaker boxes
- Elevators and related equipment
- Footings, foundations, posts, etc., required to support the building

- Fuel tanks and the fuel in them
- Furnaces, water heaters, heat pumps
- Non-flammable insulation **in a basement**
- Sump pumps; pumps and tanks used in solar energy systems
- Stairways and staircases (attached to the building)
- Water softeners and the chemicals in them, water filters and faucets (installed as an integral part of the plumbing system)
- Well water tanks and pumps
- Required utility connections for items on this list
- Clean-up

These limitations may apply in certain elevated building enclosures located in Special Flood Hazard Areas. Drywall and non-flammable insulation are not covered in Post-FIRM Elevated Buildings in the SFHA.

Basement Coverage (cont'd)

Personal Property Covered

The list of personal property items covered in a basement under Coverage B is much shorter. It includes:

- Portable or window air conditioning units
- Clothes washers and dryers
- Food freezers and the food in them

If the insured has purchased personal property coverage, the only items covered in a basement are the above three items. If it is not on this list, it is not covered in a basement.

Coverage C: Other Coverages

Debris Removal

Now we will move on to Coverage C – Other Coverages. Coverage C contains a set of miscellaneous coverages beginning with debris removal.

In severe flooding situations, it is common to have debris that the policyholder doesn't own on his or her property, or maybe the policyholder's debris has floated elsewhere. The NFIP has added coverage that would reimburse a policyholder to remove non-owned debris from on or in the insured property and retrieve and remove his or her debris from anywhere. The coverage will also reimburse the policyholder for his or her labor should the policyholder or any members of the household decide to remove the debris.

Coverage C: Other Coverages (cont'd)

Loss Avoidance Measures

Two types of loss avoidance measures are covered under Coverage C:

1. Sandbags, Supplies, and Labor

This coverage reimburses the insured for activity to reduce the flood damage. For example, if the insured attempts to protect his or her property by sandbagging, erecting a temporary levee, or purchasing and operating a pump, he or she can be reimbursed for the cost of that effort, including labor up to a limit of $1,000.

2. Property Removed to Safety

This coverage reimburses the insured up to $1,000, including the value of his or her own labor, if he or she chooses to move property to another location to protect it from the flood. In this situation, the NFIP agrees to cover the property at that alternate location for a period of up to 45 days, against the peril of flood only.

Coverage C: Other Coverages (cont'd)

Condominium Loss Assessments and Pollution Damage

In the Dwelling Form, reimbursement of condominium loss assessments is also a Coverage C item and this item can apply to assessments levied by condominium associations on unit owners in the aftermath of a flood. But take a careful look at this section of the policy as there are a number of limiting factors built into the policy language on such loss assessments.

And finally, under certain conditions, pollution damage is covered in the General Property Form—up to $10,000. This coverage does not include the testing for or monitoring of pollutants unless required by law or ordinance.

Coverage D: Increased Cost of Compliance

Coverage D, also called Increased Cost of Compliance or ICC, provides up to $30,000 of coverage to help cover the cost to bring flood-damaged buildings in compliance with the current floodplain management ordinance. If the building has been substantially damaged or in some cases repetitively damaged by flood, Coverage D will pay to:

- elevate
- floodproof (non-residential)
- demolish, **or**
- relocate the structure

Every participating NFIP community has a substantial damage provision in its flood ordinance which requires it to monitor flood damages exceeding 50% of the market value. Some communities also monitor the cumulative damages of repeat losses. In many cases, where the building is below the current elevation standards, it is clear that it would not be safe to rebuild at that level. If the building is substantially damaged, it will be required to be brought into compliance. ICC coverage is intended to help with that effort if the damage is by flood. The $30,000 limit is dedicated to just Coverage D.

NFIP Coverage Limits

There are maximum limits available through the NFIP as currently authorized by Congress. In essence, you cannot sell more than this coverage through the NFIP or a WYO company.

Currently, in Regular Program communities, the maximum limit for all one- to four-family **residential** buildings is $250,000, and contents coverage is limited to $100,000.

The maximum coverage limit for non-condominium residential buildings with five or more units (classified as **Other Residential**) is $500,000 with a contents maximum limit of $100,000.

For **Non-Residential Business and Other Non-Residential** buildings, the maximums are $500,000 each for building and contents.

Available limits for the entry-level Emergency Program communities are much lower.

Property Not Covered and Exclusions

We have mentioned a lot of things we <u>do</u> cover. Next we will discuss the sections **Property Not Covered** and **Exclusions** in the Standard Flood Insurance Policy.

Here are examples of **Property Not Covered**:

- Personal property outside the fully enclosed building
- Property in, on, or over water
- Walks, decks, and driveways
- Land, trees, shrubs
- Fences, seawalls, piers, docks
- Self-propelled vehicles, recreational vehicles
- Livestock
- Crops
- Accounts, bills, coins, currency, other valuable papers
- Underground structures and equipment (e.g., septic systems)
- Storage for gases or liquids
- Pools and equipment, hot tubs (except as bathroom fixtures)

This is just a partial list of the types of property not covered under the SFIP. An exhaustive list is featured in the policy.

Exclusions

Next we will take a quick look at some exclusions. The Standard Flood Insurance Policy only covers direct physical loss by or from a flood. This means the policy does **<u>not</u>** cover time element exposures like:

- loss of revenue or profits
- loss of access
- business interruption
- additional living expenses

Some more examples of exclusions include:

- Sewer backup/seepage
- Overflow from sump pump
- Seepage or leaks
- Damage from the pressure or weight of water

The policy excludes all of the above **unless** there is a general condition of flooding in the area and the flood is the proximate cause of those types of losses.

Deductibles

Pre-FIRM subsidized policies and full-risk rated policies have their own two-tiered minimum deductible which varies depending on whether the coverage limit is above or below $100,000.

For **Pre-FIRM subsidized rated policies**, the minimum deductible is $1,500 if the coverage is $100,000 or less but increases to $2,000 if the coverage is over $100,000.

Policies rated with full-risk rates, Preferred Risk Policies (PRPs) and Newly Mapped-rated policies have a $1,000 minimum deductible if the coverage limit is $100,000 or less, while those with over $100,000 in coverage have a $1,250 minimum. A PRP or Newly Mapped-rated policy with contents only will have a $1,000 deductible. Newly Mapped-rated policies will be discussed in Lesson 3.

Some other important features of deductibles will be reviewed next.

Deductibles (cont'd)

Higher Deductibles are Available

Higher deductibles are available up to $10,000 for residential buildings, $50,000 for Non-Residential Business and Other Non-Residential buildings, and $25,000 for condominium associations.

Separate Deductibles for Building and Contents

It should be noted that if the insured elects to buy both building and contents coverages, the policy will have two separate deductibles. When selecting the $10,000 residential deductible option, the same deductible amount must apply to both building and contents.

How Losses are Settled by the NFIP

Let us turn our attention to how losses are settled in the National Flood Insurance Program.

There are three types of loss settlement described in the Standard Flood Insurance Policy:

1. Replacement Cost Value (RCV)
2. Actual Cash Value (ACV)
3. Special Loss Settlement (for certain manufactured homes or travel trailers)

We will spend a moment reviewing the three loss settlement approaches.

How Losses are Settled by the NFIP (cont'd)

Replacement Cost Value

In order to receive Replacement Cost Value (RCV) loss settlement, the situation must fit a very specific profile.

Replacement Cost Value is the cost to replace property with the same kind of material and construction without deduction for depreciation.

The first thing you should know is Replacement Cost Value loss settlement applies only to buildings, never to contents. There is no RCV loss settlement on contents in the NFIP.

To be eligible, three conditions must be met:

1. The building must be a single-family dwelling
2. It must be a principal residence, meaning the named insured or the named insured's spouse has lived there for either 80% of the 365 days immediately preceding the loss, or 80% of the period of ownership if less than 365 days
3. Building coverage must be at least 80% of the full replacement cost of the building, or the maximum available for the property under the NFIP

How Losses are Settled by the NFIP (cont'd)

Replacement Cost Value under RCBAP

Replacement Cost Value loss settlement also applies to the Residential Condominium Building Association Policy (RCBAP).

As you may recall, the RCBAP is written in the name of the condominium association on behalf of all of its unit owners. Replacement Cost Value loss settlement applies to buildings other than manufactured homes or travel trailers when they are insured under the RCBAP. When Replacement Cost Value loss settlement applies to the building elements of an eligible condominium building, the RCBAP requires that the building be insured to value. This means it must be insured to at least 80% of the building's replacement cost at time of loss <u>or</u> up to the maximum limit available through the NFIP.

If the building is not insured to value at time of loss, it will be subject to a co-insurance penalty.

How Losses are Settled by the NFIP (cont'd)

Actual Cash Value (ACV)

Now that we have dealt with RCV, let us talk about ACV.

Actual Cash Value is Replacement Cost Value at the time of loss, less the value of its physical depreciation.

Some buildings will always be settled using an ACV loss settlement:

- Two- to four-family dwellings
- Single-family dwellings that are not eligible for RCV
- Non-Residential Business and Other Non-Residential buildings
- Detached garages
- Mobile homes under 16 feet wide and under 600 square feet

How Losses are Settled by the NFIP (cont'd)

Special Loss Settlement

There is one last loss settlement option, and it only applies to a single-family dwelling that is:

- A manufactured or mobile home or a travel trailer
- At least 16 feet wide, with at least 600 square feet
- A principal residence

If they qualify, partial losses are covered on a Replacement Cost Value basis, while a total loss is settled at the lowest of the building's policy limit, its replacement cost, or 1.5 times its Actual Cash Value.

Summary of Coverage

To quickly finish up this lesson, we will discuss the impact of the Flood Insurance Reform Act of 2004 on your policyholders. The Act requires that all carriers send the following to policyholders annually:

- Cover letter
- New or renewal Declarations Page
- Four-page Summary of Coverage

Select this link to view the Summary of Coverage. This FEMA publication provides general information about deductibles, what is and is not covered by flood insurance, and how items are valued at time of loss.

Claims Handbook

The Flood Insurance Reform Act of 2004 also requires that FEMA send policyholders the following:

- Cover letter
- Loss history for the insured property
- Flood Insurance Claims Handbook. Select this link to view the Flood Insurance Claims Handbook.
- Acknowledgement of Receipt form to sign and return

Select this link to learn more about this FEMA packet.

Lesson 2 Summary

This lesson presented an overview of important things to know about the Standard Flood Insurance Policy including:

- Basic knowledge that you can share with your policyholders regarding which policy form corresponds to each building type and what is covered
- An overview of when a flood policy becomes effective, including the 30-day waiting period
- The conditions required to meet the NFIP's definition of a flood and what is and is not covered by the Standard Flood Insurance Policy in the event of a loss

<u>For complete coverage details, select this link to refer to the Standard Flood Insurance Policy forms.</u>

The next lesson presents information on building an NFIP policy.

Lesson 3 Overview

In this lesson, we will review:

- NFIP policy considerations that affect the premium
- Definitions for subsidized and full-risk rates
- Grandfathered rating and the Newly Mapped procedure

NFIP Considerations

Community Status

The first step in building our policy is determining the status of the community. Flood insurance may be written only in those communities that have been designated as an NFIP participating community.

As a flood insurance agent, you may need to find the answers to these questions:

- Does the community participate in the NFIP?
- Which phase does the community participate in, Emergency or Regular?

NFIP Considerations (cont'd)

Once you determine that the community does participate, then you have to determine whether that community is in the Regular or Emergency Program phase. These are the participatory phases that we discussed in Lesson 1. Finally, you will need to know what flood zone the property is in.

For those of you who write your flood insurance through a WYO carrier, a lot of this process may be automated for you through your carrier's rating software.

What About My Community?

Community Status Book

Select this link to view the Community Status Book and find the status of your community's participation in the NFIP.

Building Eligibility

Once we know that the community where our building is located participates in the NFIP, we can move forward with putting our policy together. There are also certain conditions related to the building structure that apply.

- **Eligibility for coverage:** First, we have to know whether our building is eligible for coverage. Remember that it has to be a walled and roofed structure that is principally above ground and affixed to a permanent site.
- **Dwelling, General Property, RCBAP forms:** We also have to know the occupancy of the building, because that will determine not only which coverage form we will use, but also the amount of coverage we can write. (Note: The building can be a mobile home or travel trailer that meets the criteria discussed in Lesson 2.)
- **Pre-FIRM or Post-FIRM (based on initial effective date of FIRM):** We have to establish which category our building fits into: Pre-FIRM or Post-FIRM. These will be covered later in this lesson.
- **Basement or enclosure:** Finally, we need to know whether our building has a basement or an enclosure. In Lesson 2, we reviewed that basements and enclosures have limited coverage, but they also have an impact on rating.

Pre-FIRM vs. Post-FIRM

Understanding which category applies to our building is important. Let us define the terms Pre-FIRM and Post-FIRM.

Pre-FIRM

A Pre-FIRM building is a building for which construction or substantial improvement occurred on or before December 31, 1974, or before the effective date of an initial Flood Insurance Rate Map (FIRM).

Post-FIRM

A Post-FIRM building is a building for which construction or substantial improvement occurred after December 31, 1974, or on or after the effective date of an initial Flood Insurance Rate Map (FIRM), whichever is later.

Importance of Initial FIRM Date

How do you determine if a building is Pre-FIRM or Post-FIRM? Simply look at the column titled **Init FIRM Identified** in the Community Status Book.

Click here to view the Community Status Book Report for Kansas.

In the Kansas report, you can see that each of the communities listed has a different date in the column entitled **Init FIRM Identified**. That date is the dividing line between Pre-FIRM and Post-FIRM. Anything built prior to that date is Pre-FIRM, and anything built on or after it is Post-FIRM. This date never changes. It remains the dividing line even after new maps have been issued.

For example, look at the listing for the City of Overland Park, Kansas. It has an initial FIRM date of September 30, 1977, but a current map date of August 3, 2009. September 30, 1977 is the dividing line between Pre- and Post-FIRM because it is the date of the first Flood Insurance Rate Map.

Subsidized and Full-Risk Rates

To continue the discussion of Pre-FIRM and Post-FIRM, we will review the differences between subsidized and full-risk rating.

Subsidized Premium Rate. A rate charged to a group of policies that results in aggregate premiums insufficient to pay anticipated losses and expenses for that group.

Full-Risk Premium Rate. A rate charged to a group of policies that results in aggregate premiums sufficient to pay anticipated losses and expenses for that group.

Subsidized and Full-Risk Rates (cont'd)

Reform Legislation

Recent legislative reforms have impacted the rating approach for certain Pre-FIRM buildings. The Homeowner Flood Insurance Affordability Act limits annual increases for individual premiums to 18% of the premium amount.

There are some limited exceptions to the 18% increase. Some policies using Pre-FIRM subsidized rates will see their premiums increase 25% per year until they reach their full-risk premium. These include:

- Subsidized non-primary residences*
- Business properties
- Severe Repetitive Loss properties
- Substantially improved Pre-FIRM buildings

***Non-Primary Residence** *is a single-family building, condominium unit, apartment unit, or unit within a cooperative building that will not be lived in by policyholder or policyholder's spouse for more than 50% of the 365 days following the policy effective date. See General Rules Section of the NFIP Flood Insurance Manual for exceptions involving active duty military personnel who are deployed, displaced policyholders, and others.*

Rate Comparisons

Subsidized Rates

We will continue the discussion of Pre-FIRM and Post-FIRM and examine the differences between subsidized and full-risk rating.

The three buildings shown have subsidized rates. Subsidized rating has traditionally applied to Pre-FIRM buildings. As you have learned, a Pre-FIRM building is one that was built before the community's first Flood Insurance Rate Map was adopted and before the Base Flood Elevation (BFE), represented by the blue line, was established.

The BFE is simply a prediction of how high the floodwaters will get when there is a 1%-annual-chance flood. Since these buildings were already there before the BFE was established, their elevation differences are ignored in the subsidized rating approach. Because all their other rating characteristics are the same, they all pay the same annual premium (in these cases, $4,551).

Building $250,000/Contents $100,000; Single Story with no basement, crawlspace, or enclosure rates; Zone AE; $2,000 deductible for building/contents. Premiums reflect rates effective 04/01/2017.

Rate Comparisons

Full-Risk Rates

Let us change one thing about this example. We will apply full-risk rates to the three buildings. Full-risk rating has typically applied to Post-FIRM buildings.

Remember, Post-FIRM buildings in A or V zones were built in the floodplain after the first Flood Insurance Rate Map was adopted and therefore after the Base Flood Elevation was established. These buildings have to play by a different set of rules when built in Special Flood Hazard Areas. Their lowest floors must be built at or above the BFE in order to lessen the impact of future flooding.

The first building does just that—in fact, it is built well above the Base Flood Elevation. It is four feet above the BFE. Notice that its lowest floor is elevated with an enclosure containing proper flood openings to get the building to four feet above BFE. (We will discuss proper flood openings and their importance later in the course.) Observe how the full-risk rating approach favors the first building. The insured pays just $617 a year for flood insurance. Now, look at its next-door neighbor, which was built a foot below the BFE. The property owner pays $4,666—about 7.5 times as much as the building that is elevated.

Our third building is four feet below the BFE, and that property owner is going to pay more than $12,000 a year for flood coverage using full-risk rating for a Post-FIRM building.

Building $250,000/Contents $100,000; Single Story with no basement, crawlspace, or enclosure rates; Zone AE; $2,000 deductible for building/contents. Premiums reflect rates effective 04/01/2017.

Rate Comparisons

Know Your Story

It is very important for property owners to know their building's story. The only way anyone currently using subsidized rates can learn that story is to obtain a FEMA Elevation Certificate for their property. It will tell them where their lowest floor is in relation to the Base Flood Elevation. It is that elevation difference which drives the cost of flood insurance when using full-risk rates.

We will provide an overview of FEMA's Elevation Certificate and how you use it a little later in the course.

Coverage Conditions Related to Premium

Next we will dig a little deeper into the process of building a flood insurance policy. Many decisions your client makes will affect the premium, such as:

- Does your client want building coverage only, personal property only, or both?
- How much coverage is requested?
- What are the desired deductibles?
- Is the community your client lives in eligible for the Community Rating System discount?

NFIP Coverage Limits

An important topic that we discussed earlier in the course is NFIP coverage limits. The maximum coverage limits available for Regular Program communities are:

- $250,000 building and $100,000 contents for one- to four-family residential buildings
- $500,000 building and $100,000 contents for Other Residential buildings
- $500,000 building and $500,000 contents for all non-residential buildings

Community Rating System

The Community Rating System discount saves insureds money on their flood insurance premiums.

The NFIP **Community Rating System (CRS)** is a voluntary incentive program that recognizes and encourages community floodplain management activities that exceed the minimum NFIP requirements.

FEMA classifies all participating communities on a scale from 1 to 10, providing premium discounts for Class 9 or better which range from 5% to 45%. Communities receiving a CRS discount are listed in the NFIP Flood Insurance Manual. <u>Select this link to view the Flood Insurance Manual.</u>

Select this link for more detailed information on the Community Rating System.

Reserve Fund Assessment

Another item that goes into the premium calculation is the Reserve Fund Assessment. Its purpose is to set aside a fund to pay future claims.

The Reserve Fund Assessment is calculated as a percentage of the total premium, excluding the Federal Policy Fee, which we'll cover in a moment. The percentage may vary from year to year. Also, you may want to note that the Reserve Fund Assessment is not subject to agent commission.

For detailed information on the current Reserve Fund Assessment, select this link to view the NFIP Flood Insurance Manual, then go to the Rating section.

Federal Policy Fee

A mandatory annual fee called the Federal Policy Fee is also added to the premium.

The NFIP defines the **Federal Policy Fee** as a flat charge you must pay on each new or renewal policy to defray certain administrative expenses incurred in carrying out the National Flood Insurance Program.

On a Preferred Risk Policy, a lower Federal Policy Fee is charged. And for condominium associations written under the RCBAP, the fee is set by a sliding scale based on the number of units.

Select this link to refer to the NFIP Flood Insurance Manual for complete details on the current Federal Policy Fee.

HFIAA Surcharge

As part of the Homeowner Flood Insurance Affordability Act, a congressionally mandated premium surcharge is applied annually to all new and renewed policies.

The surcharge is a flat fee applied to all policies based only on the occupancy type of the insured building. This fee is not associated with the flood zone in which the building is located or the construction date of the building. It also applies to a renter's contents-only policy based on the policyholder's occupancy of the building or unit.

The surcharge is $25 for policies on primary residences or $250 for all other policies.

Primary Residence: FEMA defines a primary residence as a single-family building, condominium unit, apartment unit, or unit in a cooperative building that will be lived in by the policyholder or the policyholder's spouse for more than 50% of the 365 days following the policy effective date (or 50% or less of the 365 calendar days following the current policy effective date if the policyholder has only one residence and does not lease that residence to another party or use it as rental or income property at any time during the policy term).

A policyholder and the policyholder's spouse may not collectively have more than one primary residence.

For more details, select this link to review the NFIP Flood Insurance Manual and refer to the Cancellation section.

Rating Options Following a Map Revision

Cost of Flood Insurance

A building's flood zone is a significant factor in determining the cost of a flood insurance policy. Typically, the flood zone used for rating is the flood zone that the building is located in on the community's current Flood Insurance Rate Map. But with more and more revised flood maps being issued, more insureds are eligible to take advantage of the NFIP's "grandfather" rules or the Newly Mapped procedure. We will address both of these options in detail.

Grandfathering

Next, we will learn about the NFIP "grandfather" rules. Grandfathering allows premium benefits after:

- Changes in map zones
- Changes to compliance standards

Grandfathered rating is used in conjunction with flood map changes—it allows buildings to be rated using the flood zone from a prior map. Grandfathered rating does not change what flood zone a building is actually in, but it can change what zone it is rated in. When more favorable, some buildings can be rated based on a previous Base Flood Elevation. In essence, it allows property owners to lock in a previous flood zone or Base Flood Elevation. This is done using either the Continuous Coverage Rule or the Built-In-Compliance Rule.

Under the **Continuous Coverage Rule**, if a policy is purchased prior to the effective date of the new map, then it can be rated based on the prior map's flood zone or Base Flood Elevation. As the name implies, continuous coverage must be maintained. The Continuous Coverage Rule applies to both Pre-FIRM and Post-FIRM buildings.

The second grandfathering option is called the **Built-In-Compliance Rule**. If a building was built in compliance with the map that was in effect at the time that it was built, then the building can be rated using that map's flood zone or Base Flood Elevation. Proof must be submitted to the carrier. Continuous coverage is not required for this option. This grandfathering option applies primarily to Post-FIRM buildings.

Your Source for Previous Flood Maps

FEMA Flood Map Service Center

When documenting that a building was built in compliance, you may need to view and print a copy of prior (historic) flood maps using the Map Service Center, which we looked at in Lesson 1. <u>Select this link to visit the FEMA Flood Map Service Center</u>.

Just click on the "Search All Products" link to search for the community or jurisdiction by entering the name or via the dropdown menu. This will provide a list of the historic products, if there are any.

Rating Options Following a Map Revision

Newly Mapped Procedure

The Newly Mapped procedure applies to properties previously in Zones B, C, D, or X that have been newly mapped into a Special Flood Hazard Area (SFHA). Also, an AR or A99 zone property being mapped into a different SFHA could also be eligible. The procedure applies to Preferred Risk Policy Eligibility Extension policies issued prior to April 1, 2015 as long as continuous coverage is maintained. The Newly Mapped procedure does not apply to properties mapped into the SFHA by the initial FIRM.

**The Preferred Risk Eligibility Extension offered financial relief to policyholders by providing temporary eligibility for the Preferred Risk Policy for buildings newly mapped into an SFHA on or after October 1, 2008.*

Rating Options Following a Map Revision (cont'd)

Newly Mapped Procedure

Here's how it works. Properties newly mapped into an SFHA on or after April 1, 2015, are eligible for the Newly Mapped procedure if the applicant obtains coverage that is effective within 12 months of the map revision date and if the property does not fall under any of the categories of Ineligible properties listed in the Newly Mapped section of the NFIP Flood Insurance Manual.

The Newly Mapped procedure offers a premium identical to a Preferred Risk Policy (PRP) premium for the first year, but that's before the Reserve Fund Assessment and Federal Policy Fee are applied. The total amount paid under the Newly Mapped procedure will be a bit higher than the total paid for PRP buildings because the PRP rate tables reflect a lower Federal Policy Fee. After the first year, policies rated under the Newly Mapped procedure will transition to full-risk rates through premium increases, which are subject to the 18% annual cap discussed earlier.

Rating Options Following a Map Revision (cont'd)

Newly Mapped Procedure

Eligible properties that do not obtain coverage within 12 months of the map revision date cannot utilize the Newly Mapped procedure. Post-FIRM buildings my still qualify for built-in-compliance grandfathering while Pre-FIRM buildings may qualify for Pre-FIRM subsidized rates.

Lesson 3 Summary

This lesson presented an overview of all the basic knowledge from previous lessons to show how to build an NFIP policy including:

- The fundamental knowledge of community participation and the phase of participation help determine the maximum policy limits to offer your clients
- How Pre- and Post-FIRM buildings are classified and why it is important to understand the two building categories
- Provisions such as the grandfathering options and the Newly Mapped procedure can provide clients discounted benefits after undergoing a map change

Understanding the ins and outs of rating will assist you in explaining how much flood insurance costs.

The next lesson presents information on understanding the Elevation Certificate.

Lesson 4 Overview

In this lesson, we will review:

- The basics of the Elevation Certificate
- The Elevation Certificate's role in rating a flood policy
- The building types
- The rating elements

Client Questions

Basic information about the FEMA Elevation Certificate will be covered next. An Elevation Certificate is sometimes needed to rate the flood policy.

When asking a client to provide an Elevation Certificate, common questions posed by the client are:

- What is an Elevation Certificate? And why do I need one?
- Who certifies the elevations?
- Where can I find a qualified professional to certify the elevations?

Impact of Elevations on Flood Insurance Premiums

Rate vs. Risk

The elevation difference refers to the height of a building's lowest floor relative to the Base Flood Elevation (BFE). A building with its lowest floor above the BFE may sustain less or no flood damage, making the flood risk lower. The lower the risk, the lower the premium.

Base Flood Elevation

The Base Flood Elevation is the expected depth of the 1%-annual-chance flood. In other words, it is how high the water may rise according to the flood studies that the maps are based on.

Why an Elevation Certificate?

Let us review why we may need an Elevation Certificate. When required, it is an important aspect of policy rating. It documents the elevation levels of floors within the building and of the ground (or grades) around it. It is used to help determine the lowest floor for rating purposes and to help analyze the flood risk of a particular building. Select this link to view the FEMA Elevation Certificate.

To correctly rate a flood insurance policy, you must identify the Lowest Floor Elevation (LFE) of the building. The Lowest Floor Guide section of the NFIP Flood Insurance Manual has detailed instructions for determining the lowest floor. Select this link to view the NFIP Flood Insurance Manual.

How the Elevation Certificate is Used

The Elevation Certificate has a variety of uses:

- Agents use it to help determine policy rates
- Local floodplain administrators use it to certify building elevations and to document community compliance with its floodplain management ordinance
- It is also used to support flood map revisions or amendments

Who Certifies the Elevation?

Here is the good news—the agent does not complete the Elevation Certificate. The agent only interprets it. The Elevation Certificate is typically completed by a licensed surveyor, architect, or engineer.

You can find a qualified professional through:

- Word of mouth
- The state professional association for land surveyors. To view a listing of professional land surveyors, select this link
- The state NFIP coordinator/floodplain manager
- The local community's building permit office
- The Yellow Pages under "Surveyors"
- Web search

When is an Elevation Certificate Required?

Before we go any further in our discussion of Elevation Certificates, we will discuss when you need to have one to rate a policy since you do not always need one.

Pre-FIRM Buildings (SFHAs)

An Elevation Certificate is not required when you are using Pre-FIRM subsidized rates on a Pre-FIRM building. Using an Elevation Certificate is an option if it provides the building with a more favorable rate. When full-risk rating on a Pre-FIRM building is required, an Elevation Certificate must be submitted along with the flood application. You can find the most recent guidance in the NFIP Flood Insurance Manual or by asking your flood underwriter.

Post-FIRM Buildings (SFHAs)

For most Post-FIRM buildings, you will need an Elevation Certificate if you will be rating it in an A or V zone.

Non-SFHA Buildings

Buildings in Non-SFHAs—those in B, C, D, and X zones—do not need Elevation Certificates. That is one reason the Preferred Risk Policy is so easy to write.

Sections of the Elevation Certificate

Now that we know when an Elevation Certificate is required, let us take a closer look and break down its different sections.

Sections of the Elevation Certificate (cont'd)

Section A is entitled **Property Information.**

Items A1-A4. This section identifies the building, its location, and its owner.

Item A5. Latitude and longitude coordinates are provided by the licensed professional.

Item A6. Photographs (at least two) are required if the Elevation Certificate is being used to obtain flood insurance through the NFIP.

Item A7. The building diagram that best represents the building is selected from the diagrams shown on pages 7–9.

Items A8 and A9. Details about buildings with a crawlspace, enclosure, or attached garage. What is the square footage of those building elements? How many flood openings are located within one foot of the lowest adjacent grade? What are the measurements (square inches) of the flood openings?

Sections of the Elevation Certificate (cont'd)

Section B is entitled **Flood Insurance Rate Map Information.**

Items B1-B7. Provides information found on the FIRM panel that includes the building's location.

Item B8. Flood Zone. Remember that all zones beginning with the letter A or V are considered Special Flood Hazard Areas. This information is a key component of rating.

Item B9. Base Flood Elevation (BFE). As you may recall from Lesson 3, the Base Flood Elevation is the elevation of surface water resulting from a flood that has a 1% chance of being equaled or exceeded in any given year. When using full-risk rates, you will need this elevation to help calculate the premium.

Item B10. Source of the BFE is identified.

Item B11. Elevation datum is provided.

Item B12. Identifies Coastal Barrier Resources System (CBRS) area or Otherwise Protected Area (OPA).

Sections of the Elevation Certificate (cont'd)

Section C is entitled **Building Elevation Information (Survey Required).**

Item C1. In this field, the professional will indicate whether the elevations to be entered are based on construction drawings, a building under construction, or finished construction.

Items C2.a-d These items will assist in determining the Lowest Floor Elevation (LFE) for rating. Which elevation level will you be rating from? Remember, the LFE will be compared to the Base Flood Elevation to determine the elevation difference.

Items C2.f-g The lowest adjacent grade (ground) and the highest adjacent grade (ground) are captured here.

Item C2.h The lowest grade elevation at the deck support or stairs will be entered to support a request for a Letter of Map Amendment or a Letter of Map Revision-F (based on fill).

Sections of the Elevation Certificate (cont'd)

Section D is used for certification purposes. This section of the Elevation Certificate may be signed only by a land surveyor, engineer, or architect who is authorized by law to certify elevation information.

Sections of the Elevation Certificate (cont'd)

Section E is completed if the building is located in Zone AO or Zone A (without BFE). If not, Section C will be completed.

Items E1-E5. Measurements for top of bottom floor, permanent flood openings, attached garage slab, machinery and equipment, and specific compliance for Zone AO.

Section F is provided for certification of measurements taken by a property owner or owner's representative when responding to Sections A, B, and E.

Building Diagrams

As briefly discussed earlier, the Elevation Certificate form includes a series of 11 building diagrams which professionals use to guide them through capturing the required elevations for different types of buildings.

Select this link to view the FEMA Elevation Certificate. The building diagrams are found on pages 13-15.

Types of Buildings

Non-Elevated Buildings

We will focus on one of the building diagrams, Diagram 1A. It represents a common non-elevated building that is found throughout the country. The diagram is of a simple slab on grade building. This building has no crawlspace, basement, or enclosure—just a concrete slab.

The professional completing the Elevation Certificate will refer to the building diagrams for guidance in determining which elevations to capture. This information will be recorded in Items C2.a-h of the Elevation Certificate.

Basically, capturing all the elevation levels of the building including the top of the slab, attached garage floor, and machinery and equipment will assist you in determining the Lowest Floor Elevation for rating.

If your client's building is a slab-on-grade building, the Lowest Floor Elevation will most likely correspond to the information in Item C2.a (Top of Bottom Floor) because there is no floor lower than the slab. Of course, if we were dealing with a building with a basement, then the basement floor would be the lowest floor and would also be captured in Item C2.a.

Types of Buildings (cont'd)

Elevated Buildings

Now we will look at a different type of structure—an elevated building.

An elevated building is one that has no basement and that has its lowest elevated floor raised above the ground level by foundation walls, shear walls, posts, piers, pilings, or columns.

Elevation Certificate Diagram 5 closely resembles the buildings shown in the photograph. We see elevated buildings most commonly in coastal and lakefront areas. They are elevated above the BFE to reduce the risk and severity of flood damage.

This photograph shows that floodwater can flow freely underneath the buildings which would minimize structural damage.

Types of Buildings (cont'd)

Enclosures

What would happen if someone were to enclose the area beneath the lowest floor?

Enclosures can cause additional risk to the building and many times can increase the premium if not properly constructed to ordinance standards.

An **enclosure** is that portion of an elevated building below the lowest elevated floor that is either partially or fully shut in by rigid walls.

Types of Buildings (cont'd)

Proper Openings for A Zones

In A zones, a full enclosure beneath an elevated building is allowed. However, it must be vented to allow the flow of water underneath the building. The vents must meet certain criteria for the building to have "proper openings" as follows:

- Openings must be permanent to allow free movement of water without human intervention
- Bottom of all openings must be no higher than one foot above the higher of (a) the exterior or interior grade or (b) the floor immediately below the openings
- One square inch of opening required for each square foot of enclosed area
- Minimum of two openings is required on different sides of the enclosed area

Types of Buildings (cont'd)

Breakaway Walls for V Zones

While enclosures containing proper flood openings are allowed in A zone buildings, breakaway walls are the standard in V zones. Remember, V zones are affected by velocity wave action.

Imagine a wave crashing against a building. Would proper openings be sufficient to allow the water to flow beneath the building?

Of course not. Breakaway walls provide the ability for the enclosure wall to break away from the building.

Rating Case Study

We will tie everything together in a quick rating case study. Your client has a Post-FIRM building in Zone AE and wants $200,000 of building and $80,000 worth of contents coverage. It is a single-family dwelling with one floor and no basement.

Let us review some rating elements:

Will an Elevation Certificate be needed? Yes, since the building is Post-FIRM and in a Special Flood Hazard Area.

Your client's Elevation Certificate shows the Base Flood Elevation to be 746.2 feet, and the Lowest Floor Elevation is 747.5. Therefore, the **elevation difference** is 1.3 feet above, which rounds down to 1 foot.

You then plug that +1 elevation difference into your carrier's rating software or go to the appropriate rate table in the Flood Insurance Manual.

In addition to calculating the building and contents rates, you will add the premium for **Coverage D–Increased Cost of Compliance**. Next, add the **Reserve Fund Assessment** and then add the **HFIAA surcharge** which is $25.00 because this is a primary residence. Finally, you will add the **Federal Policy Fee**.

You have now successfully incorporated information from the Elevation Certificate into the rating process.

Lesson 4 Summary

This lesson presented an overview of the Elevation Certificate and other important rating considerations including:

- The Elevation Certificate is a tool used to capture elevations for a specific property. Two of the elevations captured, the Base Flood Elevation and the Lowest Floor Elevation, are used to calculate the elevation difference
- The elevation difference is in turn used to determine the flood risk of a building and plays an important role in the cost of flood insurance

- The building type (slab, basement, elevated building, etc.) is key in determining the Lowest Floor Elevation

Understanding these concepts will assist you in explaining the cost of flood insurance to your client.

The next lesson presents information on National Flood Insurance Program resources.

Lesson 5 Overview

In this lesson, you will review NFIP resources available to help you.

Resources for Insurance Agents and Their Clients

In Lessons 1 through 4, we discussed many resources that are available to help you write flood insurance. We have compiled the top resources below. To view each online resource, select the heading.

Flood Insurance Library

The Flood Insurance Library includes manuals, handbooks, Community Rating System resources, Community Status Book, Standard Flood Insurance Policy forms, and the Summary of Coverage publication.

NFIP Flood Insurance Manual

The Flood Insurance Manual is available in sections, or you can download the entire manual as a ZIP file.

National Flood Insurance Program website

Here you can access publications, marketing materials, and information sheets.

FEMA's Flood Map Service Center

The FEMA's Flood Map Service Center (MSC) is the official distribution center for digital flood hazard mapping products.

Lesson 5 Summary

Here are the key points discussed in this lesson.

- Where to find NFIP Resources
- Information found at the resource links
- How each resource link is useful to expand your NFIP knowledge